Mr Pot has a house.
Here it is!
It is a white house.
And it has a red door.

This is Mrs Pot. This is Mr Pot.

Here is your egg, dear.

Thank you, dear.

dear    Mr    Mrs

1

Mr Pot has paint pots.
How many?
One, two, three, four,
five, six, seven, eight.

Eight paint pots.

Mr Pot is on his bicycle.
He has eight paint pots.
And a ladder.

Goodbye, dear.

Goodbye, dear.

bicycle    goodbye    ladder    paint pot

The policeman has a house.
Mr Pot paints it yellow.

Mmmmm. Yellow!

Thank you, Mr Pot.

Mr Pot is on his bicycle.
He has paint pots.
He has a ladder.

Good bicycle.

paint

3

Mr Pot stops.
He looks at the dirty city.

"Oh!"

Mr Pot pushes his bicycle.

"This is a dirty city."

4

dirty    city

Mr Pot paints a shop.

Hello.

Hello.

White.

Good.

Red.

Very good.

Goodbye.

Thank you, Mr Pot.

Look at the houses!
They are very dirty.

Mr Pot paints the houses.

clean

Mr Pot is happy.
He paints and paints.

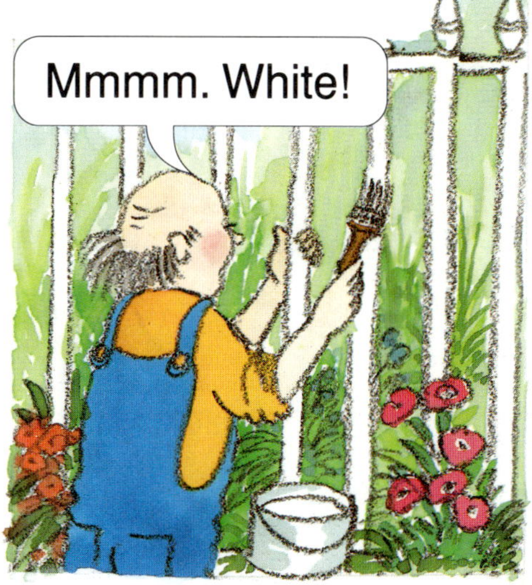

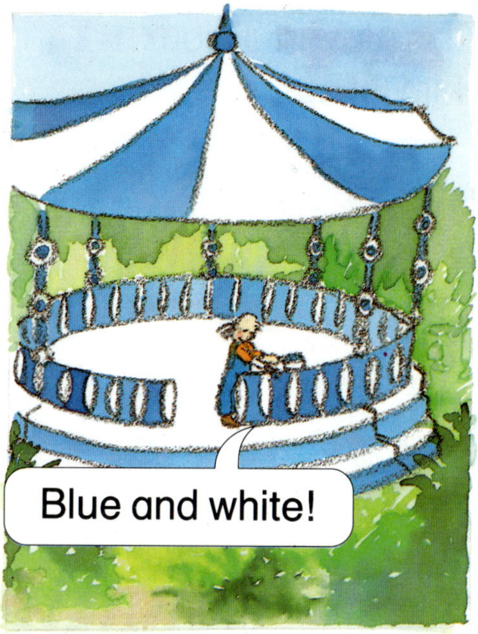

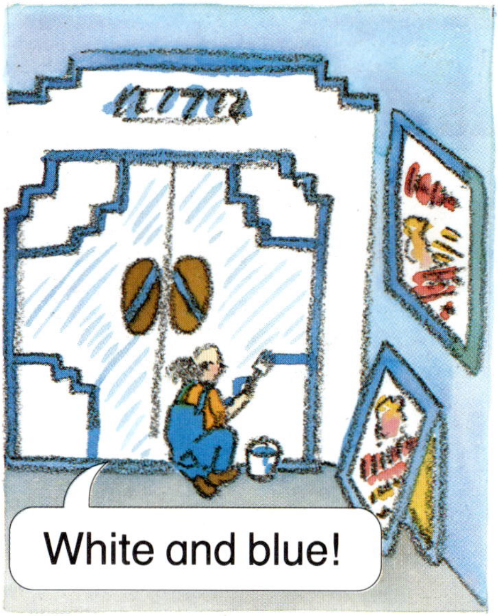

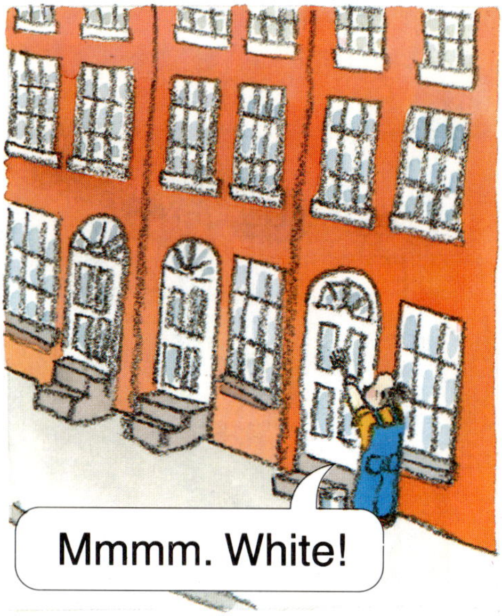

It is eleven o'clock.
Mr Pot stops.

Mmmm.
Eleven o'clock.

Thank you.

Thank you.

Mmm.
They are big.

8

Look! It's Leslie Longladder!

"Hello!"

"Hello!"

"My name is Leslie Longladder."

"And here's my long ladder!"

My name is Mr Pot.

And here are my pots!

Mmmm.

Mmm.

Mmmm.

Mmm.

10

Mmm

The buildings are big.
But the ladder is long.
It is a very long ladder.

"Please paint this building."

"This is a good ladder."

"Yes, it is."

building

11

Look at the buildings!
They are good and clean!

Thanks, Leslie Longladder.

Thanks, Mr Pot.

One o'clock.

Time to eat.

12

Look at the city!
Is it grey and dirty?
No, it is not.

Hello.

Hello, dear! This is my friend, Leslie Longladder.

Thank you, Mrs Pot.

Look at the sky.

Mmm.

sky

13

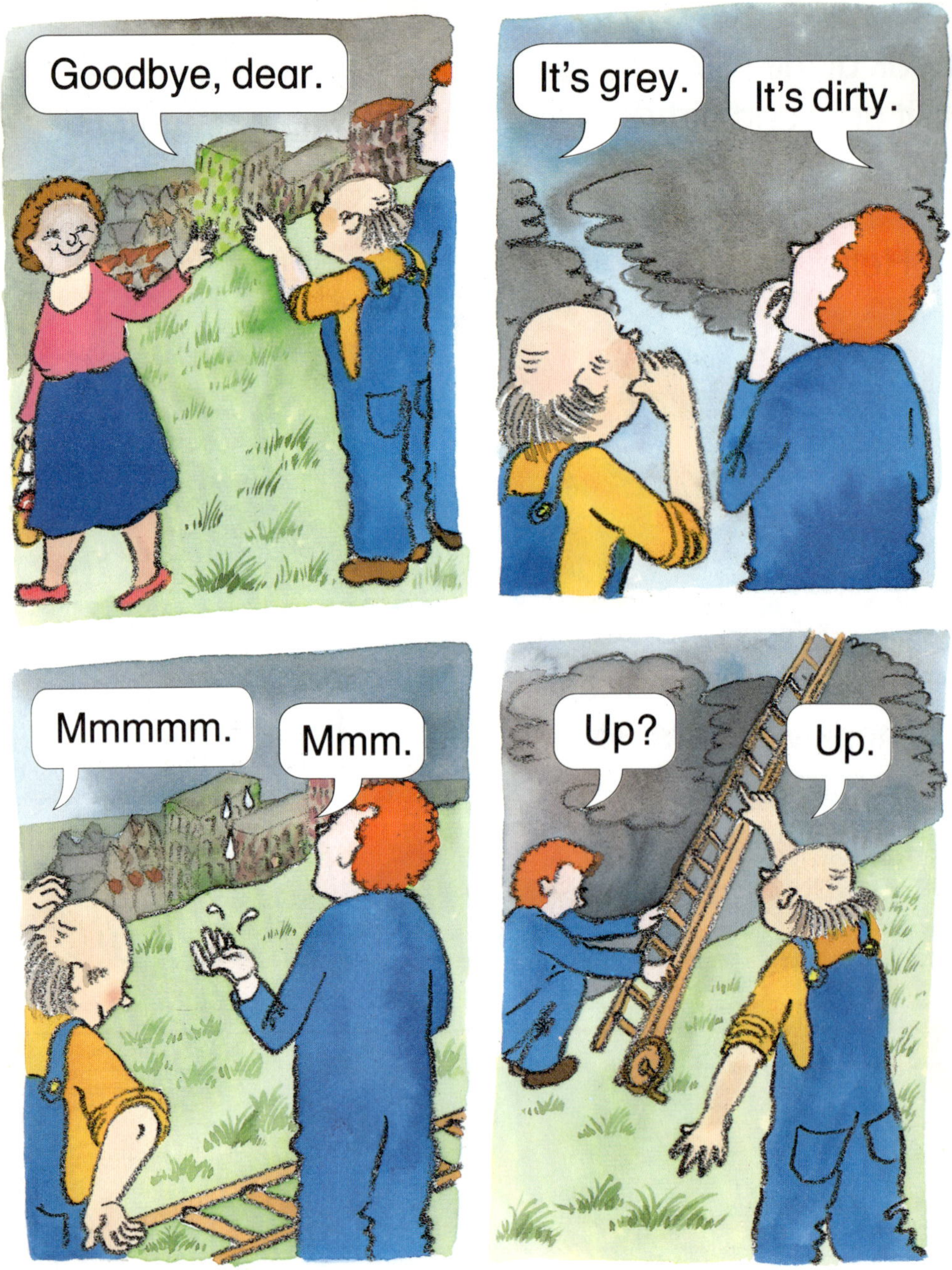
Goodbye, dear.
It's grey.
It's dirty.
Mmmmm.
Mmm.
Up?
Up.

The ladder goes up.

"Up?"

"Up."

"Paint the sky?"

Mr Pot goes up.

"Yes. Paint the sky."

Look at Mr Pot!

"Paint the sky!"

15

It is a very long ladder.

Blue.

Mr Pot paints the sky blue.

It looks good, Mr Pot!

16

It is eight o'clock.
Mr Pot paints stars in the sky.

The blue sky is clean.
And look at the stars!

Look at the ladder!

Look at the man!

Look at the sky!

Look at the man!

He's up in the sky!

Hello!

man

17

They come out of the city.
They point to the sky.

Down?

Down.

Look at the stars up in the sky!
The sky is clean and blue.
Mr Pot comes down the ladder.

Very good.

Here.

Very good.

18

come out of

It is eleven o'clock.
It's time to go.

Goodbye.

Goodbye.

Goodbye my friend!
Thanks!

Goodbye my friend!

It's twelve o'clock.
Mr Pot stands at the door.
He says goodbye to Leslie Longladder.

Words in this Book

| bicycle | 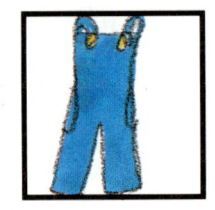 blue |  building |  city |

| clean | dirty |  come out of |  dear |

| goodbye |  green |  ladder |  man |

| Mmm |  Mr — Mrs |  paint |

20

painter   paint pot   red   sky

white   yellow

21

Questions

What colour is the house?
What colour is the door?

What is her name?

What is his name?

What colour is this?

What are these?
How many?

What is this?

22

What colour is this?
Are the buildings dirty?
Are the buildings small?

What is this?
Is the ladder long?
Is it a good ladder?

How many buildings?

What is his name?

23

Oxford University Press
Walton Street, Oxford OX2 6DP
Oxford New York Toronto Melbourne Auckland
Petaling Jaya Singapore Hong Kong Tokyo
Delhi Bombay Calcutta Madras Karachi
Nairobi Dar es Salaam Cape Town
and associated companies in
Berlin Ibadan

OXFORD and OXFORD ENGLISH
are trade marks of Oxford University Press

ISBN 0 19 422423 6

© Oxford University Press 1991

All rights reserved. No part of this publication may be
reproduced, stored in a retrieval system, or transmitted, in any
form or by any means, electronic, mechanical, photocopying,
recording, or otherwise, without the prior permission of Oxford
University Press.

This book is sold subject to the condition that it shall not, by
way of trade or otherwise, be lent, re-sold, hired out or otherwise
circulated without the publisher's prior consent in any form of
binding or cover other than that in which it is published and
without a similar condition including this condition being
imposed on the subsequent purchaser.

Illustrated by Wendy Lewis

Typeset by Pentacor PLC, High Wycombe, Bucks

Printed in Hong Kong